SUMMARY OF

REAL MAGIC

BY DEAN RADIN

WRITTEN BY
ALDEN MARSHALL

UNOFFICIAL: This summary book is unofficial and unauthorized. This book is not authorized, approved, licensed, or endorsed by either the author or the publisher of the summarized work.

All Rights Reserved. Copyright © 2020 by Alden Marshall

Note to Readers:

This is an unofficial research and reference guide to meant to enhance your reading experience of the original work with a concise summary of the key concepts. You are strongly encouraged to buy the original book if you find this useful.

No part of this publication may be reproduced, stored in a retrieval system or transmitted in any form or by any means, electronic, mechanical, photocopying, recording, scanning or otherwise, except as permitted under Sections 107 or 108 of the 1976 United States Copyright Act, without the prior written permission of the Publisher.

Limit of Liability/Disclaimer of Warranty: The publisher and the author make no representations or warranties with respect to the accuracy or completeness of the contents of this work and specifically disclaim all warranties, including without limitation warranties of fitness for a particular purpose. No warranty may be created or extended by sales or promotional materials. The advice and strategies contained herein may not be suitable for every situation. This work is sold with the understanding that the publisher is not engaged in rendering medical, legal, or other professional advice or services. If professional assistance is required, the services of a competent professional person should be sought. Neither the publisher nor the author shall be liable for damages arising herefrom. The fact that an individual, organization or Web site is referred to in this work as a citation and/or a potential source of further information does not mean that the author or the publisher endorses the information the individual, organization or Web site may provide or recommendations they/it may make. Further, readers should be aware that Internet Web sites listed in this work may have changed or disappeared between when this work was written and when it is read.

Books in the Condensed Esoterica Collection:

Some of these titles are coming soon. Please subscribe to the mailing list to be notified when they become available.

- Summary of Modern Magick by Donald Michael Kraig
- Summary of My Years of Magical Thinking by Lionel Snell
- Summary of Magical Healing by Josephine McCarthy
- Summary of Psychic Self-Defense by Dion Fortune
- Summary of Oriental Magic by Idries Shah
- Summary of Psychedelic Information Theory by James L. Kent
- Summary of The Secret Teachings of Plants by Stephen Harrod Buhner
- Summary of Occulture by Carl Abrahamsson
- Summary of Exploring the World of Lucid Dreaming by Stephen LaBerge and Howard Rheingold
- Summary of Real Magic by Dean Radin
- Summary of Quantum Enigma by Rosenblum, Bruce and Kuttner, Fred
- Summary of Visual Magick by Jan Fries
- Summary of The Apophenion by Peter J. Carroll
- Summary of Advanced Magick For Beginners by Alan Chapman
- Summary of Life Force by David Lee
- Summary of Pieces of Eight by Gordon White
- Summary of Prometheus Rising by Robert Anton Wilson
- Summary of Prime Chaos by Phil Hine
- Summary of The Trickster and the Paranormal by George P. Hansen

- Summary of SSOTBME edited by Ramsey Dukes
- Summary of DMT: The Spirit Molecule by Rick Strassman
- Summary of LSD: Doorway to the Numinous by Stanislav Grof, M.D.
- Summary of Reality Transurfing: Steps I-V by Vadim Zeland

CONDENSED ESOTERICA

BY ALDEN MARSHALL

Foreword

We live in an age where we are nearly overwhelmed by a vast wealth of information available to us: Both the treasured information of ancient texts and lengthy modern discourse on all manner of esoteric topics are available to us in a variety of physical and digital formats with the simple click of a button.

While our position may seem enviable to students and researchers of ages past, the sheer quantity of resources available and the dubious quality of many of them can make it challenging to know where to start for a dedicated and serious seeker of knowledge who is interested in understanding the truth about these complicated topics.

How does one sort truth from fiction? How does one know which of the many-hundred-page books available to spend one's precious time upon? You've surely had the all-to-familiar experience of purchasing a heavy tome about a topic you're deeply curious about, only to find many hours later that it offers little of actual value to you by the time that you're done reading. Time is our most precious resource, and we should not waste it.

My goal for the Condensed Esoterica series is to hand-pick and carefully summarize only the best and most often-recommended books on magical, spiritual, entheogenic, and philosophical practice and theory so that you can learn from the wisdom of the most experienced teachers available to us without poring over tens of thousands of pages on your own. I hope that you will find this series useful as a way to better understand the world around you and to gain insight into how you might be able to use the wisdom gained to improve your life and the lives of those around you.

This book is intended to be used as a research guide and a companion piece to the original work, as well as a reference guide and summary of the key concepts presented by the original author. I have meticulously read the original in its entirety to produce this set of notes and captured all of the key concepts and ideas from the original source to the best of my ability.

Please also consider joining my mailing list, the details of which are provided at the end of the book, so that I can inform you whenever a new volume has been added to the Condensed Esoterica collection. I welcome your comments and suggestions, and I hope that you will enjoy reading these summaries as much as I enjoyed writing them.

- Alden Marshall

Introduction to the Summary

Real Magic by Dean Radin provides fascinating insights into the modern perspective of magic and how it relates to science. The author's skepticism makes this book great for new magicians that are still trying to find their way into magic.

Radin uses practical terminology and his real experiences in laboratories to illustrate his points. These can be replicated and verified to demonstrate how real magic shapes the world we live in.

The author takes great pains to lay out his data in a way that is clear and concise to lay people.

Chapter 1: Beginning

The author starts chapter 1 by affirming that this book is about real magic, his goal is to explore real magic from an evidence based scientific perspective. He explains that real magic has three categories.

1. Mental influence over the physical world, which translates to force of will, it's associated with spell-casting.
2. Perception of distant events, that means divination, tarot cards and mirror gazing.
3. Interaction with nonphysical entities is all about theurgy, evocation and communication.

The author affirms that there is plenty of scientific literature regarding magic. He explains that after decades of experimenting with magic, now without religious bias, he arrived at the following conclusions.

1. Science is the most accurate lens by which magic can be seen.
2. The reality viewed through science is but a small fraction of what we understand.

The author explains that it's foolish to simply discard centuries of advancement and knowledge. The scientific method is powerful, concise and objective. The idea is that by analyzing magic with the scientific method it becomes a phenomenon we can understand. Terms like paranormal and supernatural become tangible concepts we can qualify and reproduce.

The author proposes two themes to explore:

1. Based in a substantial body of experimental evidence magic does exist.
2. What was previously seen as magic van evolve into a new scientific discipline (e.g. astrology, alchemy evolved into chemistry)

The new discipline might study the

psychological nature of reality, exploring what exists between mind and matter. The author affirms that even with the advent of science magic still exists, some examples are:

1. Prayer is intentional magic
2. Wearing sacred symbols is sympathetic magic.
3. Religious rituals that are ceremonial magic.
4. Books about positive thinking because they follow age-old magical principles.

The author talks about the difficulty some people have to accept that magic is real, he exemplifies this using A. J. Ayer, a British philosopher specialized in logical positivism and a hard core atheist who had a near death experience (NDE) after dying and being resuscitated his intellectual position was weakened. He became more amenable to the idea of spirits. Another example is William Friedkin, the director of the movie The Exorcist and an agnostic. To prepare for the movie he spent time with a Vatican exorcist and presented recordings of exorcisms to neuroscientists that didn't dismiss the idea. Yet another example is Michael Shermer, a true skeptical character. His bride had lost her grandfather before their wedding, he had left her a radio that didn't work. After their wedding ceremony the radio started playing a love song. The writer explains that the idea of the unknown terrifies people but these three experiences suggest that magic is always present, it can be present in many aspects of our life.

The author points out that the pursuit of real magic is motivated by power. – Power leads to wealth, to fame, to love or maybe just to sex. That's the nature of spell casting, it all depends on the magician. The morality is merely questionable when magical power is used to manipulate or exploit, that's what is called black magic. The author affirms that the use of magic to resolve conflicts, which are natural since humans are sociable creatures, violates the Golden rule and therefore it's immoral.

The author explains that prayers with the

intent of hurting someone else are black magic and shows the use of defixiones magic plainly on TV during a debate. He explains that to some people the use of magic to bind someone in order to prevent that person from making threats or harming qualifies as gray magic, he qualifies this justification as a slippery slope.

He affirms that prudence is needed when dealing with black magic because every action is followed by a consequence.

- **Theurgy:** The word Theurgy is Greek and comes from theoi, "Gods", and ergon, "work", meaning not only "Divine Work" but also "Work of God" or "producing the work of the gods". Theurgy was a term created by the Neoplatonic philosophers of the plotino current and Ammonio Sacas. It is a form of ritual (ceremonial) magic, with the aim of incorporating divine strength either in a material object such as a statue, or in the human being through the production of a visionary trance state. He seeks perfect communion with God, obtained through ceremonial techniques such as rituals, prayers, exercises and studies. It has a lot of influence on esoteric Christianity. Theurgy is known as "high magic", it is the most powerful magic that exists. In this sense, theurgy is also considered the search, the path that is traveled in magic for contact with the divine plan. For this reason, theurgy is also known as white magic or divine magic.

- **Black magic:** The term black magic encompasses a wide set of magical systems of diverse origins, traditions and cultures. Black magic is the handling of supernatural forces with malevolent intentions and purposes. The management of these forces is carried out in various ways by those who believe in their possibility and effectiveness, ranging from the performance of ceremonial complexes as well as daily symbolic gestures of malice, envy or other emotion directed negatively. Black magic can be confused with Satanism, but this is another occult system, which is concerned with the worship or making of pacts or agreements with Satan or Lucifer. Black magic is linked to the Hermeticism and has a branch originating from the ancient Jewish kabbalah called goetia, this is believed to be a magic practice that was revealed by God to King Solomon allowing him to invoke 72 angels and demons and his control to execute all their desires, through this magic it is believed to originate all the wealth and wisdom that immortalized Solomon

- **Defixiones:** These are magical practices of the Ancient Mediterranean, through the process of Roman expansion. It is used to bind or constrain the object of the spell. Defixiones have diverse purposes. Defixiones can be used to resolve legal disputes, thefts, fights.

Chapter 2: Science and Magic?

In chapter 2 the author explains that he was shocked when he realized that he was studying magic, he was formerly educated in music, physics, electrical engineering, psychology and cybernetics. Magical thinking was his first magical experience. He wished the tornadoes he frequently witnessed on his way to the university in Illinois would stay out of his path as a way to cope with the peril.

During his career he studied the relationship between three factors. The brain, the cognitive and perceptual capacities of the mind and consciousness. The third factor is the most baffling and humanity has yet to understand what is consciousness, what is its purpose and where does it come from.

The author explains that without consciousness there wouldn't be a you or me. He proposes three approaches used to study consciousness. And a fourth (4) that he uses.

1. The philosopher method is about analyzing concepts, logic and assumptions about consciousness.
2. The scientific method, scientists study brain activity and experiences.
3. Mediators study consciousness using introspection.
4. The author investigates psychic phenomena (telepathy, clairvoyance, precognition and psychokinesis) that challenge assumptions about the relationship between brain and mind.

The author explains that the connection between parapsychology and amusing tabloid stories damage the credibility of parapsychology. Because of this, parapsychology is avoided and radicalized even when it proposes a scientific approach to human experiences, we lack understanding. He reports that he joined, presided and it's still a member of the Parapsychological Association, an organization affiliated with the American Association for the Advancement of Science (AAAS). The writer affirms that after decades of lab work and publishing he accepted that psi is real because he has seen the applicability in lab experiments.

The author affirms that psi is magic and you can find studies in parapsychology in many books even if these studies avoid using terminology related to magic. The author mentions Patrick according to Patrick Dunn, another author, science can't explain magic any more than it can explain art while Gordon White, a respected writer appreciates the relevance of science when studying magic. To the author the bottom line is:

1. All conventional academic books about magic treat the subject as delusions or ancient history.
2. Psi research literature ignores magic.
3. Magic literature ignores psi.

- **Telepathy:** This is an extra sensory perception. The phenomenon can happen consciously or semi-consciously. Mental telepathy is the process of transferring thoughts from one mind to another, it has traditionally occupied the realms of science fiction or the paranormal, both of which are outside mainstream science. Telepathy is a generic term for any skill that involves the projection, reading and manipulation of thoughts. Telepathy has two categories: telepathic communication, which is the ability to transmit information from one mind to another, and telepathic perception, which is the ability to receive information. From one mind to another.

- **Clairvoyance:** This is the ability of obtaining knowledge of an event, being or object, without the use of any known human sensory channels and without the use of Telepathy. The term clairvoyance is also applied, in certain schools of spiritualism and occultism, to the "spiritual vision", which allows one to see spiritual plans or at least something pertaining to such plans. In the specific case of Spiritism, clairvoyance, double sight and second sight are synonymous. Lucidity, on the other hand, refers especially to somnambulistic clairvoyance.

- **Precognition:** This is an extra sensorial perception in which the individual perceives information about a future local or event before it happens. The precognitions of negative facts are usually more perceived than positive ones, because positive facts are so frequent in our lives that they are normal and draw less attention than facts that are out of harmony.

- **Psychokinesis:** This is the capacity of the human mind to act at a distance on objects, elements and materials. This is because, according to this theory, the energy of each one of us can transform and externalize. Directed by the mind, it would act on objects, moving and breaking them. Parapsychology scholars have conceded authentic phenomena, even though scientists still don't agree.

Chapter 3: Magical Potpourri

Magic is an interesting topic and there's plenty of material to read about it (movies, grimoires, videos, poetry, grimoires, mythologies and fiction). It's a popular field, there are many best-sellers and award-winning movies about the subject. Some examples are, The Little Prince, Alice in Wonderland, The Lord of the Rings and Harry Potter.

There are many academics involved in the study of occulture, a term coined by Christopher Patridge religious studies professor. The author talks about esoterism and peer reviewed scholarly journals. He mentions an article focused on Jewish love magic from the Societas Magica Newsletter. Love magic is an ancient category of magic. Love spells are meant to attract partners, separate lovers or even gaining favor. Every spell reflects the culture it is inserted in. A Jewish spell would read differently from a Greco-Roman love spell.

The author affirms that from a scientific perspective, magic provides many clues about who and what we are and our capabilities. It is part of religion, whether theists accept it or not, symbols are sympathetic magic, they represent a connection between deity and guru. The promise of magical powers is seductive, even London muslims are susceptible to the allure, some of them are interested in the ruqya shariya, a healing practice.

From a negative perspective, magic can be terrifying because it lacks the boundaries that keep things in order in a society. Real magic challenges everything important and individual, it challenges sovereignty, privacy and secrecy. Magic offers the ability to read thoughts, manipulate health, emotions and even finances, the idea that you don't have control over these matters is terrifying.

The author explains that even religious faith requires the belief in magic, catholic priests are allowed to perform the sacrament of the Eucharist. It was difficult for the church to distinguish miracles and diabolic magic which led to the condemnation of any form of magic. The author talks about how some books like Harry Potter and The Hunger Games were banned by religion because of their ties to witchcraft and Satanism.

The writer explains that magic has been marginalized and the prejudice against it made it develop much slower than other sciences. With the development of other sciences supernatural concepts were outdated and left behind, the same happened to religion. This change made scholars reject magic because it was the past of scientific concepts, anthropologists played a big part in this practice, Sir Edward Brunett Tylor, the first anthropology professor at Oxford University believed that magic was merely a delusion. Many anthropologists after him thought that the presence of magic belief in other cultures was evidence of primitive men. Not all anthropologists agree with Tylor, Michael Winkelman was one of the professionals that published an article stating the opposite.

Despite the disbelief about magic women are still killed in many countries for being accused of witchery. The author affirms that magical thinking is one of the magical actions more performed in the world, it can be beneficial even if you're not aware of what you're doing.

- **Ruqya shariya:** This is a lawful incantation meant to combat black magic, cure the evil eye and even physical ailments. It is based on the recitation of Quran, remembrance and supplications.
- **Eucharist:** This is a term which means "give thanks". This word took on a new and profound meaning when Christians began to call the Last Supper celebrated by Jesus "Eucharist". In the Catholic Church, the Eucharist is one of the seven sacraments. For the Catholic Church, the Eucharist is the memorial of Christ's Easter, the updating and sacramental offering of his sacrifice, in the Church's liturgy which is eating his body and drinking his blood. This, of course, is symbolic.
- **Magical Thinking**: This is the belief that certain thoughts would lead not only to the fulfillment of desires, but also to the

prevention of problematic or unpleasant events. Magical thinking involves several elements, including the belief in the interconnectedness of all things through forces and powers that transcend physical and spiritual connections. Magical thinking involves special powers and forces in many things that are seen as symbols.

Chapter 4: Origins of Magic

Chapter 4 is dedicated to the study of the origins of magic, the author explores magic from the earliest recounts we have to how we understand magic today.

Our ancestors classified everything they didn't understand, which means basically everything, as magical or supernatural. Naturally humans began to notice the predictability of what was around them, sun, stars, plants and animals. Natural magic turned into science and today we understand electricity, fire, the microscopic nature of diseases.

In a lengthy and detailed chapter, the author discusses in a thorough review, the history of science, religion, philosophy and metaphysics of esoterism and magic. The author starts his review studying the axial age, the establishment of religions such as Taoism and Confucianism in China and prophets like Isaiah and Jeremiah in Palestine. Greek philosophers and the meaning of humanity, mathematics and rationalism. The author talks about Plato and Eleusinian mystery schools. An example of mystery school initiate is Plato, known to this day for his allegory of the prisoners in a cave. His teachings gave birth to Neoplatonism. Neoplatonism opened the door to the possibility of magic.

The Middle Age (or the Dark Age) a period that spawned from the fall of the Roman Empire to the beginning of the Renaissance is known for being dangerous for pagans, the Catholic Church established the Inquisition to combat heresy and started witch hunts. The author talks about the bad blood between Gnostics and Catholics that culminated in the massacre of an entire city.

The Renaissance was the period where the printing was invented, this created an upheaval in politics, religions, economics and scholarship. This period was filled with religious reformers such as Martin Luther. The Hermeticism was created in the renaissance, the Church labeled it as heretic teachings because in their conception all humans had a spark of divine within. The appearance of manuscripts (e.g. Ficino's translation Corpus Hermeticum, published in 1945) that could potentially change the course of religion were barred by the Protestant Reformation which eliminated magical rituals popular in Catholicism (e.g. Eucharist), the hermeticism was forced to retreat once again. Elements of the Kabbalah were added to Hermeticism.

The author calls The Enlightenment the period of rapid advancement in science, technology, philosophy and politics. During these periods there were rumors about secret fraternities that combined concepts from Hermeticism, Gnosticism, the kabbalah, the Greek Eleusinian Mysteries and Egyptian lore. Two examples are the Masons and the Brotherhood of the Rosy Cross.

In the era Post-Enlightenment Isaac Newton introduced his theories to the world but he also contributed to the esotericism studying among other esoteric arts, alchemy. The author talks about scholars that were influenced by the fact that one of the smartest men in the world believed in alchemy.

During the Information Age the author mentions six notables that contributed to the magical theory. He talks about some aspects of their contributions and lives. Two examples are: Alesteir Crowley, a nonconformist that sought to naturalize magic based on the influence of science. Violet Mary Firth also known as Dion Fortune, was a member of the Hermetic Order of the Golden Dawn but left to found a new magical order called the Fraternity of the Inner Light.

The author affirms that in the Internet Age there is a lot of information about magic, this has led to a change in how it is performed and the development of scientific magic.

- **Axial age:** Historical axis, understood in the 8th to 2nd century BC, is considered a landmark in humanity, it was in this period when important principles and guidelines of life were established, seen as still in force today. In the axial period there was the emergence of monotheistic faith and knowledge based on reason.
- **Neoplatonism:** This was a philosophical, metaphysical and epistemological current of

Platonic encouragement, which developed during the Roman Empire crisis of the 3rd and 4th century and addressed philosophical and religious issues. The first philosophers to argue for Neoplatonism were Plutarch, Maximus and Aesidemo, however, it was Plotinus who synthesized the thinking of those philosophers in his work, he divides the world between the invisible and the phenomenal, from which the first would contain the aspects "One" responsible for emanating the eternal and perfect essence (Nous) to produce the soul of the world.

- **Inquisition:** Pope Gregory IX instituted the so-called Inquisitio haereticae pravitatis, which would become known as the Court of the Holy Inquisition. This court was guided by the canonical code of the Church and, in its regiment, there were also principles of the legal code of the Holy Roman-German Empire, at the time commanded by Frederick II. The inquisition was created to prosecute crimes of heresy, recurring in the 13th century.

- **Gnosticism:** This designates a set of beliefs of a philosophical and religious nature whose basic principle is based on the idea that there is an immortal essence in each man that transcends man himself. Gnostics consider human existence in this world to be natural, as it is subjected to various sufferings. According to Gnosticism, the path to freedom from these sufferings is through knowledge. Not knowledge acquired in a rational and scientifically based way, but intuitive and transcendental knowledge that gives meaning to human life itself.

- **Kabbalah:** This is a word of Hebrew origin that means reception. It is the mystical aspect of Judaism. It is a religious-philosophical system that investigates the divine nature. It is the mystical aspect of Judaism. There are historical indications that sages and alchemists formed "Brotherhoods" for the study and practice of Kabbalah. The word itself means: From mouth to ear, that is, knowledge transmitted orally. Until the Middle Ages, when a disciple came to know some of his secrets, he had to swear not to reveal the mysteries to profane ears, as this knowledge was kept under lock and key.

- **Masonry:** This consists of fraternal organizations that date back to local bricklayers' fraternities that, since the 14th century, regulated the qualifications of their profession and their interaction with authorities and clients. Freemasonry maintain the three degrees of medieval craft guilds, those of "apprentice", "companion" and "master Mason". The candidate of these three degrees is taught the meanings of their symbols and is entrusted with greetings, signs and words to indicate to other members that he has been initiated.

Chapter 5: Practice of Magic

Chapter 5 is dedicated to magic practice; the author affirms that a practitioner needs to have attention and intention when performing magic. Magic is modulated by belief, imagination, emotions and clarity. There are many theatrical aspects to rituals and magic, they're overall unnecessary but they add to the experience. The author explains that the most important magical skill is to enter in gnosis, a state of consciousness. Your results depend on the force of will and force of will magic depends on attention, intention, imagination and more importantly belief. To perform it you need to:

1. Know what you want.
2. Review your goal daily.
3. Maintain secrecy.
4. Strengthen your belief.

The author talks about sigils, he explains that sigils require more focus and the use of symbolic goals. The author informs that sigil does work frequently enough to be interesting. He explains that he has encountered synchronicity in several stances, he talks about each incident and explains the context behind these situations. The author supposes that intense intention might warp some aspects of reality and cause synchronicity.

To make a sigil you need to:

1. Write your wish.
2. List the letters ignoring the vowels.
3. Fit the letters together to form a symbol.
4. Focus on the symbol, project your emotions on it, and charge it by engaging in physical or sexual activity.
5. Release your attention away from the sigil.
6. Keep in mind your belief.

The author talks about Divination, a practice also known as clairvoyance. The method demands that the practitioner draws an abstract sketch of impressions the magician receives about a location, object or person. Another technique the author mentions is the Remote Viewing Training, the author drew a ritual step by step for the readers, and the eight steps are as follow:

1. Hold the target in mind and sketch whatever comes to your mind.
2. List the sensory impressions you had, odor, taste, touch, sound, visual impressions, shape and even color.
3. Examine the target from different perspectives.
4. Make a note about any emotional feelings you might have.
5. Combine all the information you gathered about the target, write what you think the target is.
6. Review your work. Try to gather more information or have an insight.
7. Compare the sketch of the target with your final descriptions.

The author punctuates a few divination tips that the parapsychologist Rhea White reported to achieve better results. He punctuates the need for relaxation, mind stabilization and redirection, wait in expectation and look for conviction.

- **Sigils:** This is a type of symbol used in magic. In the medieval magical ceremony, the term secrecy was commonly used to refer to hidden signs that represented various angels and demons that the magician could summon. In magic, Sigil acts like a code that acts directly on the magician's subconscious. Simply put, Sigils are synthesized representations of the will transcribed in a simple and direct way.
- **Synchronicity:** This is a concept developed by Carl Gustav Jung to define events that are related not by causal relationship but by meaningful relationship. The concept refers to two events, interior and exterior, which occur simultaneously without having a connection that can be rationally explained, however, that have meaning for those who are watching.
- **Divination:** This is the act or effort to predict things distant in time and space, especially the

uncertain outcome of human activities. Divination is present in many cultures and traditions, it determines the meaning or hidden causes of events, predicting other people's thoughts, thoughts or feelings, changes in their future lives, through varied practices of consulting the oracles.

Chapter 6: Scientific Evidence

The author talks about the existence of psi phenomena from a scientific perspective. He explains that there are a lot of experiments and researchers dedicated to studying these sciences, he emphasizes the fact that even though science is not as partial when it comes to funding. He talks about the application of theurgy in laboratories. The author affirms that statistics is an important discipline to evaluate experimental data and understand the evidence on psi.

The author talks about the six-sigma threshold, studies that have overall odds over a billion to one. These experiments are protocols used to avoid known design flaws. The six experiments are:

1. Telepathy
2. Remote viewing
3. Presentiment
4. Implicit precognition
5. Random number generators (RNGs)
6. Global Consciousness Project

The author affirms that other studies that aren't up to the six-sigma level may do so after they have collected enough data from experiments on human physiology and behavior.

The author explores how some aspects of magical lore were studied. The author explores the experiments on force of will, how belief modulates performance and how divination works. He discusses the results in each experiment proposed and details the results, combing through theories with the readers and assessing theories in the literature.

The theories can be resumed in:

1. A study on the relationship between Quantum Consciousness and Force of will, where the author mentions that some scholars believe that someday we'll be advanced enough to detect the interaction between these two variables in laboratory experiments. He cites some experiments that tried to achieve this objective. The author details other relevant RNGs experiments performed. The results

suggest that in order to achieve a positive result you need to give it an honest try.

2. A series of experiments he performed with his colleagues, in this experiment he described seventeen experiments using double-slit optical systems.

3. The author talks about the act of blessing food or even water, Catholics perform it in the ritual of the Eucharist, the priest becomes the instrument through which the Holy Spirit transforms wine into blood and bread into the body of Christ. Blessing food is a magical expression of will. Another common way to bless food is to express gratitude for an animal sacrificed or a harvest. The author reports his double-blind experiment to test the beneficial effects of a blessing on dark chocolate, three methods were used to bless the chocolate and the results can be explained as a fluke.

4. The author reports yet another experiment, this time with blessed water, the results suggested that when objectively measurable force of will does change the plant growth. The author affirms that it's necessary to plan your goals. One way to accomplish something according to magical lore is to act as if it's been already accomplished. The author proposes a baseball metaphor to illustrate this. The author explains that the goal in replicating this experiment is to check if intention influences chance. The experiment is complex and the author explains the results on random decisions with random RNG. He discusses the results obtained and explains the figures of the experiment performed.

5. The divination experiment is based on the idea of an absolute future; it ignores the existence of free will. The author questions whether precognition perceives

a future that will happen or a future that will probably happen. To check this the author uses cards in an experiment similar to the ESP test by J.B. Thine in 1930. The results suggest that the probabilistic influence detected is an unconscious tendency

6. The author questions whether the esoteric concept of world soul can be measured. The author mentions the Global Consciousness Project, a project that investigates the collective effect. In this project the RNG was used to produce random bits, the results showed that collective mental coherence can cause a disturbance.

7. The author also talks about how we sometimes have the feeling of being stared at. The author reports that an experiment performed on this subject validated with meta-analysis wielded interesting results.

8. The writer details an experiment on voodoo healing practices that was successful when performed under strict vigilance.
9. The writer talks about theurgy studies on various fields, near death experiences, flat lined electroencephalograms (EEG), hallucination, mediumship. He explains some of the experiments performed and published. The writer talks about the many grievances that being open to magic turned their job into a difficulty. The author talks about the assumption that consciousness is generated by the brain, and how neurosciences showcase the correlation between cognition and consciousness.
10. The author talks about mediumship, he mentions four mental states that a performer needs, recollection, perception, fabrication and mentorship.

- **Law of Correspondences:** This is one of the Seven Universal Hermetic Laws. Derived from the writings of Hermes Trismegisto, the seven principles embrace the universal essence present in all religions. The principle of Correspondence concerns the patterns - hidden or not - present in all the planes on which we walk. According to this law, the study of the microcosm can help to understand the macrocosm, as there is a correspondence between one relationship and another.

- **Transubstantiation:** This is the conjunction of two Latin words: trans (beyond) and substantia (substance), and it means the change of the substance of bread and wine in the Body and Blood of Jesus Christ in the act of consecration.

- **Anima mundi:** This is the concept of a shared soul that governs the universe by which divine manifests itself in laws that are capable of affecting matter and the hypothesis of an immaterial force, inseparable from matter, but which provides it with form and movement.

- **Tonglen:** This is a meditative practice taught by the Dalai Lama and widely used in Tibetan Buddhism. It aims to purify the person who practices and the others to whom he dedicates.
- **Haitian Voodoo:** As practiced in Haiti and by descendants of the black diaspora in the United States, South America and Africa, this is a religion based on ancestral spirits and patron saints. Haitian Voodoo was born from the mixture of Catholicism and the spirituality of West and Central Africa. In addition, scholars claim that religion was influenced by fugitive slaves who, under a common spiritual identity, wanted to inspire rebellions. In contemporary Haitian society, Voodoo works in several ways. An important contribution is your role in healing.

Chapter 7: Merlin-Class Magicians

In chapter 7 the author recalls individuals that performed advanced magical acts in front of thousands of witnesses. The author quotes some of the experiments performed in their book.

1. St. Joseph of Cupertino was poor and born during chaotic times, crippled at five he spent much of his childhood confined to the bed and into his head, fantasizing about things. He survived a surgery but was considered a simple child due to his lack of exposition to people. When he felt in trance, he gained the nickname Boccaperta (Gaping mouth), Cupertino was ordained at twenty-five years old. Joseph would perform various miracles, like blinding someone from disobedience, levitating, healing, telepathy, precognition, prophesying and many others. He was set free by the Inquisition squad the first time

he was brought up to question but was eventually sent into house arrest. After his death he was canonized.

2. Daniel Dunglas Home was born two centuries after Cupertino, in Scotland. He was a sensitive weak child but performed extraordinary psychic talents, his magical feats were studied by science and even the most knowledgeable historian of psychology, illusionist and inner magic circle member was puzzled by the acts. The magician was very famous but he also attracted many skeptical people like the Dutch rationalists. Even digging unbelievers never found a single evidence of fraud.

3. Ted Owens was born in 1920, isn't as well known as the other two but it's fairly interesting. Owen's grandfathers performed psychic games with the Ouija, to find lost objects, dowser or predict deaths. Owen changed the weather and

called in UFOs. He was bitter about the government dismissal of him.

Chapter 8: Toward a Science of Magic

In chapter 8 the author talks about the properties of psychic phenomena, he draws six conclusions based on all the scientific evidence about psi phenomena.

1. We're capable of gaining information beyond the limitation of space of rime.
2. The general population is capable of performing in Psi capacities.
3. Effects can arise from unconsciousness but can also happen during conscious awareness.
4. Psi effects are stronger during mediation, dreaming or under the influence psychedelics.
5. We're capable of mentally influencing the physical world.
6. It is possible to gain information from nonphysical entitics.

A scientific view adopts key assumptions, about realism, objects from the physical world have real and complex properties independent of observation (taste, warmth, flavor, state). When it comes to locality, in order for object A to affect object B, something or someone should exercise force in object A or B to make them collide. The second law of thermodynamics generates causality. These create the four principles of the scientific worldview responsible for the advancement that humanity has had:

1. Mechanism, everything can be understood
2. Physicalism, everything has real properties that exist in an ordinary space and time logic
3. Materialism, everything (mind and consciousness included) consists of matter and energy.
4. Reductionism, everything exists inside a hierarchy of smaller objects.

The author talks about the idea of a mystical

cosmology that birthed the religious traditions of our world, each religion is affected by cultural, socio-political and linguistic factors which is why they are so different. When we focus on the similarities of these religions, we find three simple ideas.

1. Consciousness is primary.
2. Everything is interconnected.
3. There is only one consciousness.

The author explores idealism and rationalism when it comes to understanding the universe. He proposes a model that explains why divination, force of will and theurgy work based on the assumption that consciousness and Universal Consciousness share the same composition. Following that the writer proposes a sketch of reality with three major variables, Physics, Consciousness and Symbolic language, classical physics is linked to conscious, quantum physics to subconscious and sub quantum to gnosis. He explores these ideas in the text. He proposes theories of the working between these parameters, he proposes 7 possible interpretations about the physical reality.

1. Reductive materialism, matter and energy organize themselves in ways that produce consciousness.
2. Reductive materialism, matter and energy organize themselves in ways that produce the illusion of consciousness.
3. Soft idealism, consciousness is fundamental and matter emerges out of consciousness.
4. Hard idealism, consciousness is fundamental and matter is merely an appearance within consciousness.
5. Straight-up dualism, consciousness and matter exists but neither are a product from the other.
6. Wishy-washy monism, consciousness and matter are two different sides of the same coin.
7. Cynical nihilism, neither consciousness nor matter exist.

According to these interpretations the author explores the nature of reality according to mathematicians and physicists. He presents theories and evidence that support or dismiss them such as Newton's gravitational theory and the hierarchy that sustains all that science understands until this very moment. The author presents different perspectives of philosophers on materialism and reality in a cohesive text complete with quotes of relevant books.

- **Perennial Philosophy:** This is a single, underlying mystical cosmology from which all of the tremendously diverse religious traditions of the world have emerged. Perennialism has its roots in the Renaissance interest in Neoplatonism and its idea of the One, from which all existence emanates. It is a perspective on modern spirituality that sees all religious traditions in the world as sharing a single truth, whether it is metaphysical or the source from which all esoteric and exoteric and doctrinal knowledge unfolded.

- **Idealism:** Idealism is the philosophical current that defends the existence of only one reason, the subjective. By this approach, the subjective reason is valid for every human being, in any temporal or physical space. From idealistic thinking, reality comes down to what is known through ideas. There is also a difference between reality and the knowledge we have about it. In German idealist doctrine, the power of reason is reinforced to show reality as something absolute and an object of reflection. Idealistic thinking was inaugurated by Plato. The Greek philosopher sums up idealism in the Cave Myth. In the allegory, he asserts that the shadows of the sensory world must be overcome by the light of universal truth and reason. Kant's transcendental idealism is based on the fact that knowledge is not the result of a neutral experience. Hegel, although an advocate of idealism, criticized Kant's ideas. The thinker states that the transformation of reason and its contents is driven by reason itself. He said that the reason is not in the story because it is the story.

- **Rationalism:** The main objective of rationalism is to theorize the way of knowing human beings, not accepting any empirical element as a source of true knowledge. For rationalists, all the ideas we have originate from pure rationality, which also imposes an innate conception, that is, that ideas have innate origins in the human being, being born with us in our intellect and being used and discovered by the people who make better use of reason. Descartes, Spinoza and Leibniz are considered rationalist philosophers.

- **Decoherence:** Quantum decoherence is a phenomenon that can bridge the world governed by quantum mechanics and the world governed by classical mechanics. The quantum mechanics required that matter can be in more than one physical state at the same time. This entanglement makes these more complex objects decay to a single state. Decoherence is a kind and noise, or interference, disrupting the subtle interrelationships between quantum particles. When it enters the scene, a particle that was at point A and point B at the same time suddenly becomes point A or point B.

- **Panpsychism:** This is any doctrine or belief that believes that all matter, however small, is endowed with individual conscience.

Chapter 9: Concluding Thoughts

Chapter 9 the author dedicates to concluding his thoughts on reality. He affirms that to most practitioners, magic is subtle and not as strong as fiction portrays it because:

1. Reality inertia, unconscious or merely lack of talent play against the magician. Reality reacts to intention but it is also elastic and interconnected, the rebounding effect happens when intention warps the universe for you and as a result of your actions someone else suffers from a distortion.
2. It's difficult to enter gnosis and gnosis is where magic happens. Its necessary practice and natural talent to achieve it.
3. The last factor is that you might think you want something but unconsciously you don't want what you're wishing for.

The author proposes that one day humanity will be able to create robot systems with self-awareness and consciousness. These beings would have the advantage of having better control over their psyche. These robots will outperform us and be able to practice powerful magic, following that he proposes that civilization will develop a rational scientific basis for magic and applied technology making us capable of shaping reality at will. He extrapolates the dangerous implications of that.

The author also talks about extra-terrestrials beings that are capable of manipulating space and time simply because they're more advanced than we are. He also reports that national security had contact with psi phenomena, the author questions whether the existence of psi is still controversial or is simply an uncomfortable truth.

The author affirms that people that practice esoterism, especially meditation will eventually have to choose between transcending into enlightenment or not. Enlightenment happens when your consciousness realizes that it is the Universal Consciousness. The author affirms that many scholars and even science are starting to understand that consciousness is fundamental and this brings attention to esoterism and the reality of magic.

Afterword

I hope you found this Condensed Esoterica summary to be a succinct and useful guide to the key concepts of this classic book. **If you enjoyed reading it, please leave it a review!**

In time, my hope is to provide the most comprehensive and carefully abridged library of esoterica available anywhere in the world, so that students and searchers alike can accelerate their path to learning more about these interesting and challenging topics.

Below you will find the full list of current and upcoming titles offered in my Condensed Esoterica series. Please be sure to join my mailing list to be informed whenever new titles become available, and also I would invite you to listen to the Condensed Esoterica partner podcast, Chaotic Thinking, for more illuminating conversation on these topics!

- Alden Marshall

ALDEN MARSHALL

Follow our Mailing List for Updates

Be sure to subscribe to our mailing list to continue your learning and to be notified whenever a new summary is published.

You can copy-paste this address into any browser URL bar:

https://mailchi.mp/a3d382f3c9a2/condensed-esoterica

Further Reading

Some of these titles are coming soon. Please subscribe to the mailing list to be notified when they become available.

- Summary of Modern Magick by Donald Michael Kraig
- Summary of My Years of Magical Thinking by Lionel Snell
- Summary of Magical Healing by Josephine McCarthy
- Summary of Psychic Self-Defense by Dion Fortune
- Summary of Oriental Magic by Idries Shah
- Summary of Psychedelic Information Theory by James L. Kent
- Summary of The Secret Teachings of Plants by Stephen Harrod Buhner
- Summary of Occulture by Carl Abrahamsson
- Summary of Exploring the World of Lucid Dreaming by Stephen LaBerge and Howard Rheingold

- Summary of Real Magic by Dean Radin
- Summary of Quantum Enigma by Rosenblum, Bruce and Kuttner, Fred
- Summary of Visual Magick by Jan Fries
- Summary of The Apophenion by Peter J. Carroll
- Summary of Advanced Magick For Beginners by Alan Chapman
- Summary of Life Force by David Lee
- Summary of Pieces of Eight by Gordon White
- Summary of Prometheus Rising by Robert Anton Wilson
- Summary of Prime Chaos by Phil Hine
- Summary of The Trickster and the Paranormal by George P. Hansen
- Summary of SSOTBME edited by Ramsey Dukes
- Summary of DMT: The Spirit Molecule by Rick Strassman
- Summary of LSD: Doorway to the Numinous by Stanislav Grof, M.D.
- Summary of Reality Transurfing: Steps I-V by Vadim Zeland

Recommended Podcast:

Chaotic Thinking by Liminal Warmth

Curious about mysticism, spirituality, the paranormal, or the occult? I highly recommend our partner podcast Chaotic Thinking, where occult researcher Liminal Warmth dives deep into all of these topics and more with fascinating interviews to explore the reality of all things magical, spiritual, and supernatural!

Listen now on iTunes, Spotify, and all major podcast providers.